"Learn to Tie a Tie with the Rabbit & the Fox"

Written by Sybrina Durant

Illustrated by Donna Marie Naval

"Learn To Tie A Tie With The Rabbit And The Fox"

Gift For Boys In The Wedding

Soft Cover Print ISBN-13: 978-1537559315 , ISBN-10: 1537559311
Soft Cover Print ISBN-13: 978-1-942740-13-1, ISBN-10: 1-942740-13-1

BISAC Codes:

JUV000000— JUVENILE FICTION / General
JUV012030—JUVENILE FICTION / Fairy Tales & Folklore / General
JNF001000—JUVENILE NONFICTION / Activity Books
EV100 EVENT / Wedding
TP054TOPICAL / Gift

League City, Texas, United States of America

Contact Sybrina@sybrina.com.

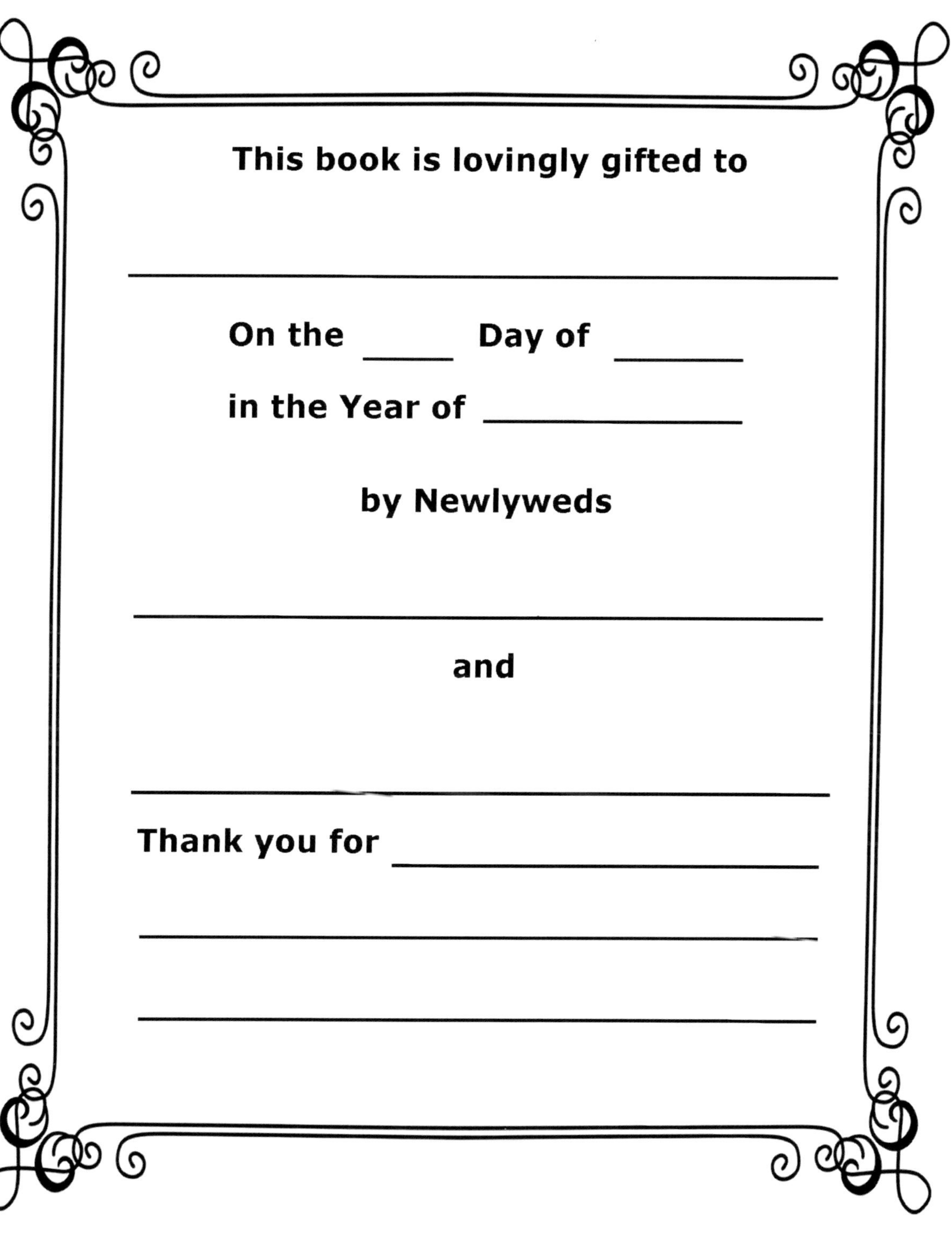

This book is lovingly gifted to

____

On the _____ Day of _______

in the Year of ______________

by Newlyweds

____

and

____

Thank you for ________________________

____

____

This book teaches how to tie a "school boy" knot through mnemonics or the art of memorizing something by associating it with words, phrases or sentences which have been especially designed to help you REMEMBER.

The Little Rabbit got away!!
Pull the blade through the neck loop.

With a giant leap, the
Little Rabbit cleared the
top of a big round log....

Tie a Tie with the Rabbit and the Fox

Song Lyrics

Rabbit and the fox,
Rabbit and the fox.
Sing along to tie a tie with Rabbit and the Fox
Rabbit ran around the tree, fox was close behind
Round the tree, they ran again, one more time.

Oh! where could rabbit hide?

Then quick, under a bush, the Little Rabbit fled
Only keeping one step ahead.
Then Rabbit took a giant leap, and he barely
cleared the top of a big, round log.

That poor Fox. . .

He could only watch as the Little Rabbit dove
to the safety of his cool, dark hole.
Rabbit and the Fox,
Rabbit and the Fox.
And that's the way you tie a tie with Rabbit
and the Fox.

Listen to this song at Sybrina.com

Dear Reader:

As an independent author, I must rely on a little help from my friends to spread the good word about my books to others.

If you like the rabbit and fox series of educational books for children or adults, please request them in libraries, schools and book stores in your neighborhood.

Plus, tell your friends in person and online. Before long everyone will be talking about the book and singing "That's the way you tie a tie with rabbit and the fox", in every language and in every country.

Your voice will make a world of difference.

Thanks for your support,
Sybrina

Trying to shake the persistent Fox, the rabbit scooted under a bush.
Push the blade under the neck loop.

The Fox, being too large, lost time struggling to follow the rabbit under the bush.

Once around the tree, the fox chased the rabbit.
Wrap the blade completely around the tail.

Twice around the tree, the Little Rabbit fled with the quick gray Fox close behind.
Repeat the last step.

In the late evening, he would come out and forage for some juicy shoots and tender morsels to eat.

One afternoon, the Little Rabbit strayed farther away from the safety of his home than he normally did.

The Little Rabbit enjoyed sleeping in that nice, cozy place, far from the rays of the blazing sun.

At the base of a large tree, he discovered some of the tenderest, juiciest shoots he had ever tasted.

For a moment, the Little Rabbit froze, his tiny heart pounding like a big fist in his chest.....
KERTHUNK!
Kerthunk!
KERTHUNK!
KERTHUNK!

He stood still as a statue as a quick gray fox surveyed the possibilities of having a tender rabbit for his own dinner.

Gathering his senses about him, the rabbit bounded away with the fox snapping at his cotton tail.
Drape tie around neck with the wide end (the blade) 12" lower than narrow end (the tail).
12"

And that's the way you tie
a tie with Rabbit and the Fox!

There you have it! In 6 easy steps, you'll look like this guy.

Twice around the tree, under a bush, over a log, into the hole and the necktie is tied!
Once your necktie is neatly knotted, you will look fantastic!

Sybrina Publishing

Exercises in manual dexterity build self-esteem in children. Knowing how to tie shoe-strings, neckties, scarves or any other knot is a useful and rewarding skill. But it can be quite challenging to master. Sybrina Durant takes the seemingly complicated task of tying a necktie knot and makes it fun and simple for both boys and girls. Her charming "Rabbit and the Fox" series of books will delight children and their parents. These books are not meant to be passive reads. Kids are encouraged to grab a tie or scarf and while reading, use it to follow the moves of the fox chasing the rabbit through the forest. The satisfying end result of this stimulating activity is a neatly knotted necktie or scarf. For a great bonding experience, get the whole family involved in learning how to tie!

ISBN# 978-0-9960940-2-3 (SC)
ISBN# 978-0-9729372-3-8 (HB)

ISBN# 978-0-9729372-7-6 (SC)
ISBN# 978-0-9906537-0-7 (HB)

ISBN# 978-0-9729372-5-2 (SC)
ISBN# 978-0-9906537-1-4 (HB)

Visit Sybrina.com to learn where to buy the books in all ebook formats plus soft cover or hard back print. Listen to the accompanying song for free!

ISBN# 978-0-9891572-2-3(SC)
ISBN# 978-0-9906537-4-5 (HB)

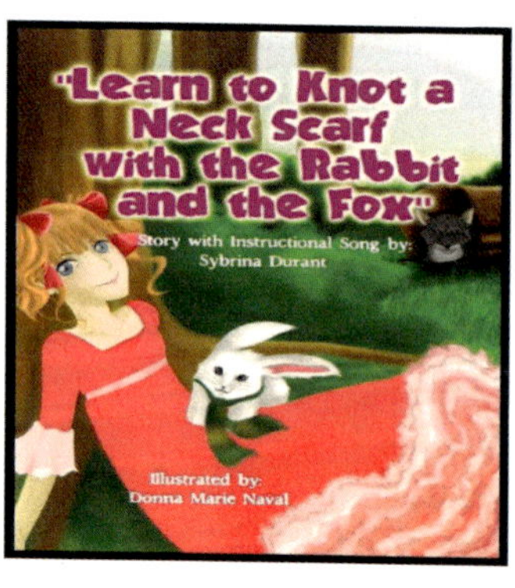

Visit http://www.sybrina.com/index_Sybrina_Publishing_Children_Stories_Retail_Catalog.htm to view entire children's book catalog from Sybrina Publishing.

ISBN# 978-0-9906537-6-9 (SC)
ISBN# 978-0-9906537-7-6 (HB)

Books may immediately be purchased at any online bookstore in soft cover (SC) or hardback (HB). They are also available in all ebook formats. Visit Sybrina.com to access links for purchasing the books from stores like Amazon, Barnes and Nobles, GooglePlay, Itunes and more. Note: If the books are not available on store or library shelves, they may be requested from any bookstore or library associate. Just provide the ISBN number for any book format listed above to a store clerk or librarian and they will order the books. Bonus! Listen to the Rabbit and the Fox song for free at Sybrina.com in English, Spanish or Tagalog. You'll find yourself singing right along.

Made in the USA
Monee, IL
08 November 2024